FLYING HIGH

THE STORY OF GYMNASTICS CHAMPION
SIMONE BILES

MICHELLE MEADOWS · illustrated by EBONY GLENN

A WHO DID IT FIRST? BOOK

HENRY HOLT AND COMPANY
NEW YORK

Simone is on the move,
watch her go, go, go!

Climbing up, dangling down,
swinging high and low.

Yet four siblings struggle.
They lack proper care.
The future's uncertain;
fear hangs in the air.

The children are placed
in a foster home,
with warm meals to eat
and a yard to roam.

Soon Grandpa arrives—
a welcome surprise.
Simone takes a trip
with hope in her eyes.

Climbing up shoulders,

bouncing off walls.

Flipping on the couch,

tumbling through the halls.

Tip, top, trampoline,
jump toward the sky.
One little girl wants
to fly, fly, fly.

As time carries on,
the siblings must split—
an impossible choice
to create the right fit.

Down at the courthouse,
adoption complete.
A family forever—
a promise so sweet.

The girls get excited
for an outdoor trip.
But rain's coming down—
drip, drip, drip.

They need a new plan to
switch the destination.
Their brother suggests
the perfect location.

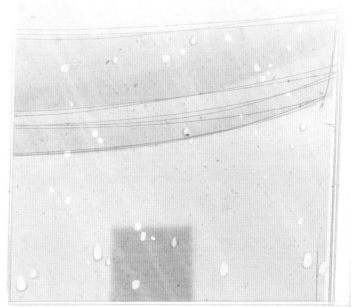

High bars, low bars,
leap across the beam.
Simone copies their moves
and launches a dream.

Level by level,
she's moving up fast.
Shooting off the vault
like a rocket blast.

After one special meet,
Simone's family grows:
now a puppy to love
with a big, wet nose.

From vault to bars,
on floor and beam—

she sets her sights on
the national team.

She comes so close,
in the fourteenth slot,
missing the team
by only one spot.

Crushed by defeat,
she loses her spark.
What will it take to
rise from the dark?

Uplifted by love,
pulled into the light,
Simone rediscovers
the magic of flight.

Back in the gym,
heavy rope to climb.
Harder routines
and more practice time.

She makes sacrifices
on the path ahead—
giving up high school
for homeschool instead.

Determined to win,
she prepares for the meet.
Shake, shake, shimmy,
tumble to the beat.

She loops and swoops,
and hears the crowd roar.

She whips and flips
and takes a top score.

Rising up through the ranks,
there's more work to be done.

With her drive to compete,
gymnastics is fun!

And what does she do
when something goes wrong?

She gets back up
and finishes strong.

Fearless and focused,
she aims for her goal.

Improving consistency,
gaining control.

Her signature move shows
phenomenal flair:
two breathtaking flips
high up in the air.

Simone is on a roll,
watch her go, go, go!
She's the best in the world
three years in a row.

At the Olympics
on TEAM USA.
Her proud family cheers!
Final Five on display.

With fire inside
that sets her apart,
Simone captures her dream
and America's heart.

GOING FOR THE GOLD: SIMONE BILES'S OLYMPIC JOURNEY

Photograph by Nathan Lindstrom

Simone Biles and her family. From the top left: Ron Jr., Adam, Simone, Adria, Nellie and Ron Biles.

Birthdate: March 14, 1997

Height: 4' 8"

Growing Up with Family: As a young child, Simone spent time in foster care with her biological siblings Adria, Ashley, and Tevin. When Simone was six and Adria was four, they were adopted by their biological grandfather Ron and his wife, Nellie Biles. Ron and Nellie became their dad and mom. Simone and Adria grew up in Spring, Texas, with their parents and two older brothers, Ron Jr. and Adam. While Ron and Nellie raised Simone and Adria in Texas, Ron's older sister raised Ashley and Tevin in Cleveland, Ohio.

Introduction to Gymnastics: Another important event unfolded when Simone was six. Simone and Adria's day care planned a field trip to a farm, but it rained. Their brother Adam worked at the day care and suggested they instead go to Bannon's Gymnastix in Houston. It didn't take long for a coach to notice Simone's natural talent. Their mother enrolled Simone and Adria in gymnastics lessons soon after the field trip.

Coaches: Simone has worked with many coaches. Aimee Boorman was remarkably influential and acted as Simone's main coach through the 2016 Olympics. Coach Boorman helped Simone get the attention of Martha Karolyi, who was the US women's gymnastics national team coordinator at the time. For the 2020 Olympics in Tokyo, Simone trained with Coach Laurent Landi. Sports psychologist Robert Andrews helped Simone cope with the pressure of competing.

Wikipedia Commons

Gold Medalist Simone Biles at the 2016 Olympics in Rio de Janeiro.

2016 Olympics in Rio de Janeiro, Brazil: Simone took home four gold medals—vault, floor, individual all-around, and team all-around—as well as a bronze medal on beam.

Making History: Simone is one of the most decorated gymnasts in history. She is the first female gymnast ever to win three World all-around titles consecutively—in 2013, 2014, and 2015.

In 2018, the International Gymnastics Federation added "The Biles" vault to the women's code of points. The vault move involves a roundoff, a half-twist onto the vault table, and a front double full somersault. Also included in the code of points is Simone's signature floor move known as "The Biles": a double layout with a half-twist landing. Simone continues to make history with her record-breaking moves, including a triple-double on floor and her double-double dismount on the balance beam.

SELECTED SOURCES

"73 Questions with Simone Biles." *Vogue.* September 15, 2016. https://www.vogue.com/article/simone-biles-73-questions-zac-efron.

Barron, David. "Aimee Boorman Redefines Coaching Relationship with Simone Biles." *Houston Chronicle.* July 16, 2016. https://www.houstonchronicle.com/olympics/article/Aimee-Boorman-redefines-coaching-relationship-8382626.php.

Biles, Simone. "Courage to Soar: Olympic Gymnast Simone Biles Says It's Not Easy Being Gold." Interview by Rachel Martin. *Weekend Edition Sunday*, NPR, November 20, 2016.

Biles, Simone, with Michelle Burford. *Courage to Soar.* Grand Rapids, MI: Zondervan, 2016.

Fishman, Jon M. *Simone Biles.* Minneapolis: Lerner Publications, 2017.

Hardy, Michael. "Gold Rush." *Texas Monthly.* July 2016. https://www.texasmonthly.com/the-culture/simone-biles-olympic-gymnast/.

"Simone Biles at Home." WTHR. May 12, 2016. YouTube video, 5:05. https://www.youtube.com/watch?v=NCte7wP1R-8.

For my husband, Rich Meadows,
who appreciates sports and the beauty of family.
—M. M.

To Simone: Thank you for inspiring so many,
including myself, to fly high.
—E. G.

Henry Holt and Company, *Publishers since 1866*
Henry Holt® is a registered trademark of Macmillan Publishing Group, LLC
120 Broadway, New York, NY 10271
mackids.com

Library of Congress Cataloging-in-Publication Data
Names: Meadows, Michelle, author. | Glenn, Ebony, illustrator.
Title: Flying high : the story of gymnastics champion Simone Biles / Michelle Meadows ; Illustrated by Ebony Glenn.
Description: First edition. | New York : Henry Holt and Company, [2020] | Includes bibliographical references. |
Audience: Ages 4–8. | Audience: Grades 2–3. | Summary: "A lyrical picture book biography of Simone Biles,
international gymnastics champion and Olympic superstar" —Provided by publisher.
Identifiers: LCCN 2019037068 | ISBN 9781250205667 (hardcover)
Subjects: LCSH: Biles, Simone, 1997–Juvenile literature. | Women gymnasts—United States—
Biography—Juvenile literature. | Gymnasts—United States—Biography—Juvenile literature.
Classification: LCC GV460.2.B55 M45 2020 | DDC 796.44092 [B]—dc23
LC record available at https://lccn.loc.gov/2019037068

Our books may be purchased in bulk for promotional, educational, or business use.
Please contact your local bookseller or the Macmillan Corporate and Premium Sales Department at
(800) 221-7945 ext. 5442 or by email at MacmillanSpecialMarkets@macmillan.com.

First edition, 2020 / Designed by Angela Jun
The artist used Adobe Photoshop to create the art for this book.
Printed in China by Hung Hing Off-set Printing Co. Ltd., Heshan City, Guangdong Province

9 10 8